Good
Lies
for
Ladies

by

Helen Ashwill

*We hope this book will enhance
your golf game & the fairways
of your life.*

Published in the United States by

Great Quotations Publishing Company
1967 Quincy Court
Glendale Heights, IL 60139

Printed in Hong Kong

*Ladies,
let's do golf.*

*Let's abandon
the malls and
the office one or
two days a week
and have a
round of golf!*

So, how shall we begin? With a new outfit of course!

The pro-shop might be just the place to get it all together. Ask around the local golf course and you'll get tips as to where the best buys are. Your new outfit will probably consist of a t-shirt, shorts or golf skirt, golf shoes and socks. Choose natural fabrics that can breathe.

These items and sun visor
or golf hat should be
coordinated in colors
flattering to you. You'll need
a good golf glove and a pair
of golf shoes, too.

After making sure it's all
pretty...make sure it's really
comfortable.

If you're comfortable -
you're confident.
If you're confident -
you'll play better golf.

"Who would you rather watch golf? A bunch of wrinkled old men or me?"

-Florence Descampe

Golf balls come in colors, too. Pink balls are a tad too much. Orange is good. White is the preferred way to go. Buy a couple dozen of the same brand of balls at your nearest discount store. Put your initials on every one with a laundry marker.

Golf Trivia:
As early as 1900 colored balls were used to play on snow covered courses.

"What's wrong with making golf a life long commitment? Why not? I love what I do. Why not continue to do what you love to do if you're successful at it and get some enjoyment out of it? Even if you're not as successful as some people think you should be, who cares?"

- Kathy Whitworth

Notice :
Your ball has dimples.

These tiny indentations trap air-
air moves more quickly over the top of the ball than around the bottom -
an aerodynamic principle which causes your ball to rise.

You see, you've nothing to worry about.

"Golf has no age limit. You can play it as long as you wish."

-Patty Berg

Of course you'll need clubs:

A driver to tee off with -
This club has a wood, metal
or graphite club face. Use
this for distance, it does not
provide loft.

Choose a 3 wood or 5 wood
for greater accuracy
although these clubs do not
allow the same distance as a
one wood or driver.
A set of long irons -
3, 4, 5, & 6 irons.

Typically they are used for distances of over 140 yards.

A set of short irons – 7, 8 & 9. These clubs are used for shorter distances of less than 140 yards from the hole.

The loft increases with the number of the iron.

Higher flight ≠ less distance.

A putter-
They don't come with the set
of clubs, but you'll need one
to get the ball in the hole!

Only putters will have grips
that are flat on top.

Golf Tip:
Croquet style putting is
illegal, so don't use it.

Golf Etiquette:
While golf is a social game,
remember to be quiet on the
tee and on the putting green.
It certainly is appreciated by
your partners and it also
enables you to keep your
concentration level up.

Let's see now...clubs,
balls, outfits, what
else?
Ah...lessons.
Do take lessons.

"*For most golfers there is a never ending struggle to improve and to learn the secrets of this complex sport.*"

-Betsy Rawls

Take lessons from a professional.
He's the Pro and do practice what he preaches at the driving range.

One professional told her student to hit four hundred balls between each lesson, *practicing the techniques she had prescribed. Sounds daunting doesn't it ?*

Yet it is really just about four buckets of balls at the range.

*"I've shown I can win.
I don't think I have to
prove myself...the girls
out here take themselves
much to seriously. I want
to have fun, fill my life
with thrills and
excitement. I'm just not
going to spend all my
time on the practice tee."*

-Laurie Davies

You can't rush your swing. You must practice. Your swing will begin to feel natural to you.

Attend golf clinics.

You may happily accept playing tips from friends but do so with a smile and a grain of salt. Remember, amateurs teach amateurs to play like amateurs.

"Using your head means being aware of the mental game of golf. Concentration does affect your shots.

If your mind is on the problems you left at the office or what the kids are doing at home, it will be hard to score well."

–Shirli Kaskie

(from A Woman's Golf Game)

The great Babe Didrikson Zaharias could hit a ball 260 yards when she began to play golf.

Babe had great upper body strength. Most women don't.
If you can't hit a long ball, hit a straight ball.

"When you can do anything to help somebody else through your sport, well, I think that's what I like about it."

-Patty Berg

Play a smart game.
Use strategy.
Plan to hit from
point A
to point B
to point C.
Yes, you are supposed to
have some control over that
little ball.
You are going to try hard to
give it direction and
purpose.

(Gee, that sounds a bit like
raising children.)

And, like children, your golf ball may take a dramatic unplanned for curve to the right or left.

"Show you want to win. Show you want something! It's so sad. It's very, very sad if you're just out there for the money. To be remembered for being second, that's the worst."

-Helen Alfredsson

"It moved!"

- anonymous golfer as she watched her ball fall from the tee as she addressed it.

Let's tee up and play golf. Approach the first tee, put that little wooden peg in the grass, set the ball firmly on top of it and straighten up.

To address the ball:
take your stance,
ground the club.
Technically you haven't
addressed the ball if you
haven't grounded your club,
placing it a few inches
behind the ball.

Mentally check off all the
things your Pro taught you
With shoulders relaxed,
bend from the hip joint at
the top of your thigh,

let your arms hang
naturally,
flex knees slightly,
keep your eyes on the ball
and swing!

Terrific feeling isn't it?

Walking proudly back to
your partners and hearing
them exclaim, "Your hair
looks great today!"

"*Any woman who can dance can easily learn the footwork of a golf swing.*"

-Marlene Floyd

Remember, from off the
tee, down the fairway to
the putting green (finally)
and down (plunk)
into that little hole that
had a flagpole stuck in it
at such a jaunty angle ...
you've got to keep your
eye on that particular
ball.
It is yours ...
and you mustn't hit
anybody else's ball.

One day your ball may even land in a bunker or sand trap.

If you choose not to use a sand wedge, a pitching wedge can be used.

*"Chipping is feel.
A lot of it can't be
taught."*

- Amy Alcott

Hit about 2 inches
behind your ball,
underneath,
to scoop it out.

Sand Wedge:
extremely lofted club with
wide flange which slices the
club head through the sand.

Etiquette Tip:
Always rake your footprints
smooth and replace divots.

Now let's get that ball down the fairway and onto the putting green.

Here is your big chance to use your putter.

"The putting stroke is the golf swing in miniature."

-Jerilyn Britz

Don't be too aggressive in your putting.
Stroke the ball, let it die at the hole. It just may roll in.

Feel a pendulum stroke ... equal distance for backswing and follow through.

Address the ball with eyes directly over the ball.

Keep head, eyes, and body still during the stroke.

"If I'm going to have any chance of making this putt, I've got to do certain things."

- Kathy Whitworth

You can make up for your fairway mistakes if you learn to putt.

Say to yourself, "I'm going to hit this toward the hole." Don't let tension freeze you. Briefly review your strategy, then just hit it!

If your ball rolls short of the hole, pick it up and mark the spot with the marker button on your golf glove or a plastic ball marker.

Now your ball is out of harm's way, none of your playing partners will hit it with their ball, costing you a penalty.

Touring pros always mark their ball and lift it to clean it off and check for spike marks or divots.

"Hitting the ball solidly is the key to playing golf well. And so often that's what a woman doesn't do when she has to hit a special shot."

-Judy Rankin

Now at last, everyone in your foursome has putted in the hole, picked up her ball and walked off the green.

Golf Tip:
Don't forget to put the flag in the hole before moving on to the next tee. Check around the green for other clubs you may have placed there before putting.

Congratulations! You've completed a hole.

Golf Etiquette:
Leave the course in better shape than you found it.

Golf Trivia:
Patty Berg, Babe Didrichson, Betty Jameson and Louise Suggs founded the LPGA in 1950.

You have to keep score as you complete each hole - so write down the total number of strokes on your score card.

Honestly?
Yes, you've got to do it honestly!

It's easy to become so preoccupied advancing your ball you lose track of your stroke count (especially in the early days when you may have several strokes to count).

To be a scrupulous and squeaky clean keeper of your own game, consider buying a prayer bead counter to tie to your belt or a wristwatch type counter.

Each player calls her own score.

This is, after all, a game of ladies and we all wish to be accurate.

"*Golf can be a good way to take your mind off the pressures of a career. It can be a formidable challenge or a way to relax. It can be a fine way to spend some time by yourself, working through the confusion and problems of daily life. It can be a source of togetherness for the entire family.*"

-Nancy Lopez
(from Nancy Lopez's The Complete Golfer)

GLOSSARY

Back Nine -
holes 10 thru 18 on an 18
hole course.

Bad Lie -
ie: a ball buried in tall grass.

Birdie -
one under par for a hole.

Bogey -
one over par.

Bunker -
an elevated or depressed
area of grass or sand.

Casual Water -
water that collects in a
low-lying area after a heavy
rain.

Divot -
uprooted patch of grass due
to your club hitting the
ground before it hits the ball.

Front Nine -
holes 1 - 9 on an 18 hole course.

Good Lie -
ie: a ball on top of the grass.

Handicap -
system that subtracts strokes from the scores of poorer players so people of different skill levels are able to compete more equally.

Hook -
a shot that veers to the left.

Lie -
the position of the ball on
the ground.

Par -
estimated standard score for
a hole based on length of the
hole and on the number of
strokes a first class player
would expect under normal
conditions to play the hole
to completion.

Slice -
a clockwise spin violently to
the right.

Yips -
nervous reaction causing
your stroke to be a jerk or a
twist.

Things to keep in your golf bag:

*Extra balls and tees
and extra ball markers,
golf glove,
insect repellent,
sunscreen, sunglasses,
a pencil for scoring,
a small towel,
a water bottle,
band-aids.*

*Here we are, back in the cart,
marking our score card and
heading for the next hole.*

*You've found your pace and
tempo now... you tee up,
wiggle your toes to relax,
focus on the ball and tee off.*

Terrific feeling isn't it?

*Knowing your partners are
watching your every move
and admiring your new
golf hat!*